THE ALL NEW STYLE OF MAGAZINE-BOOKS

SDM

www.SDMLIVE.com

MP

MOCY PUBLISHING
WWW.MOCYPUBLISHING.COM

Printed by CreateSpace, An Amazon.com Company

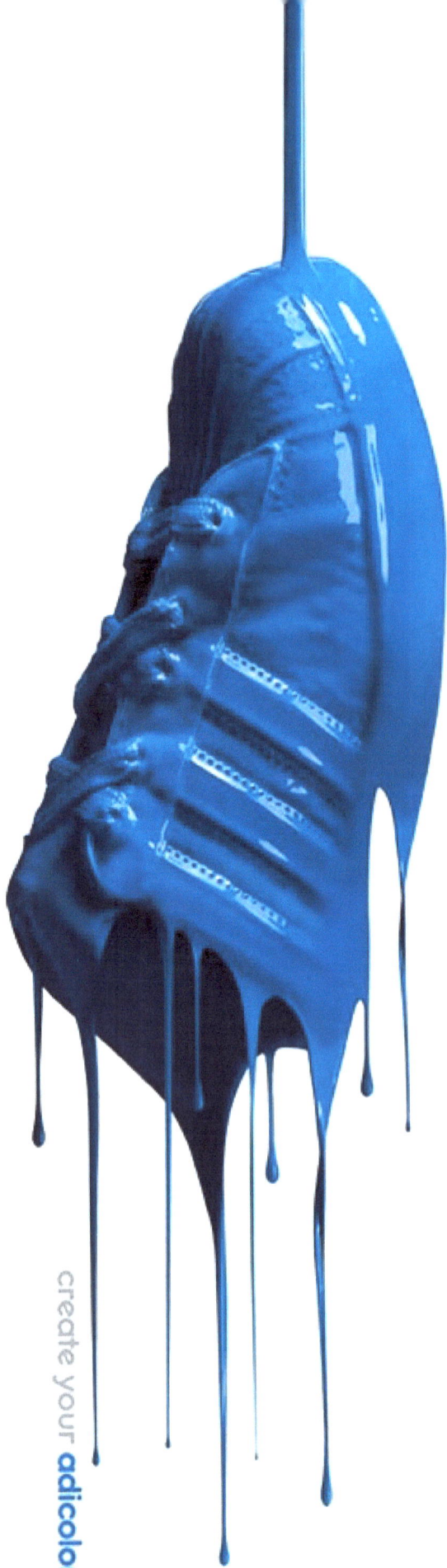

create your **adicolor**

adidas

SDM

EDITOR-IN-CHIEF
D. "Casino" Bailey
casino@sdmlive.com

EDITORAL DIRECTOR
Sheree Cranford
sheree@sdmlive.com

GRAPHIC/WEB DESIGNER
D. "Casino" Bailey
casino@sdmlive.com

A&R MANAGER
Aye Money
ayemoney@sdmlive.com

ACCOUNT EXECUTIVE
Frank Harvest Jr.
frank@sdmlive.com

PHOTOGRAPHERS
Treagen Colston
D. "Casino" Bailey

CONTRIBUTORS
April Smiley
Courtney Benjamin

COPY ORDERS & ADVERTISING OFFICE
Send Money Order or Check to:
Mocy Publishing
P.O. Box 35195
Detroit, Michigan 48235
(586) 646-8505
advertise@sdmlive.com

Copy Order Item #:
SDM Magazine Issue #2 2015
S&H Plus Retail Price - $9.99 per copy

WWW.SDMLIVE.COM

Printed by CreateSpace, An Amazon.com Company

REAL MUSIC. REAL ENTERTAINMENT.

SDM

ISSUE 3

ALSO
AUHMAZ!N
ISHMAELSOUL
MZ. PLATIUM
KIDJAY

KOSTA
JUST HIT THE JACKPOT
WITH A NEW SMASH
HIT SINGLE "LOTTERY"

BIGG DAWG BLAST
LAUNCHES THE STREET
HITTA DJ'S MOVEMENT

Neisha Neshae

BRINGING IN 2016 ON STAGE
WITH THE KING OF R&B R-KELLY
& DROPPING A NEW MIXTAPE

THE RED CARPET EDITION
SUPERSTARS CAME WITH FASHION AT
THE SDM MAGAZINE RELEASE PARTY

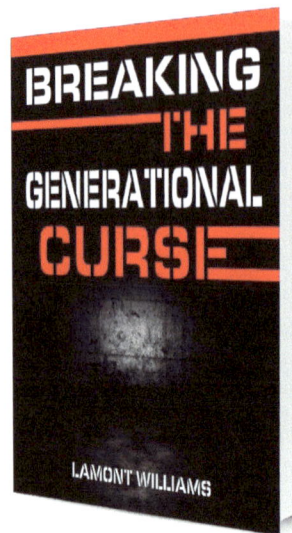

CONTENTS

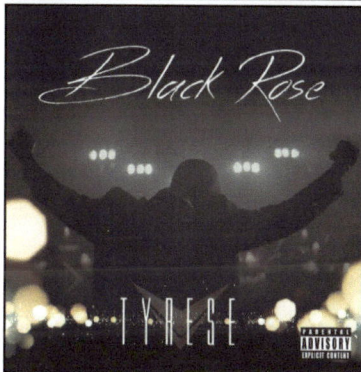

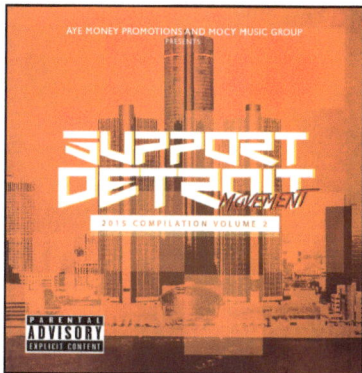

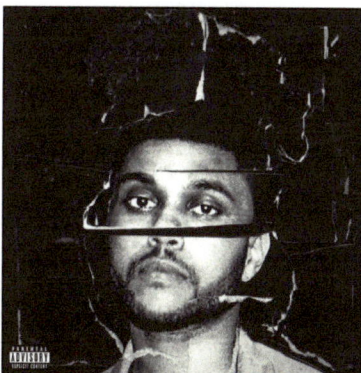

1

Microsoft - Xbox One Elite $499.99
www.bestbuy.com

**Harman Kardon
Onyx Studio 2** $199.99
www.harmankardon.com

2

3

3DR - Solo Drone $999.99
www.bestbuy.com

4

**GoPro - HERO4 Silver
Action Camera** $399.99
www.gopro.com

ASPIRE
THE BUSINESS OF BUSINESS

* List Your Company
* Attract More Customers
* Refer Other Members
* Earn 70% Commission

Become a member and save up to 50% on products and services from other members in the network.

Also earn cash by signing up other members. We offer our affiliates the highest earnings, up to 85% commission on each membership referral.

THE BEST
BUSINESS DIRECTORY
IN THE WORLD.

visit us: www.aspirebiz2biz.com

LIST YOUR BUSINESS FOR FREE LIMITED TIME OFFER!

SDM Magazine Release Party

IT WAS A NIGHT TO REMEMBER AT THE FIRST SDM MAGAZINE RELEASE PARTY IN DETROIT MI AT THE MUSIC HALL JAZZ CAFE.

by Casino B.

The event of the year in Detroit Michigan on December 17th was fabulous. While all the artists came out dress to impress for the red carpet, promoters Donna Banks, Aye Money, Chero Shanna, and Casino Bailey greeted each guest at the door.

The event included live performances, vendors, and networking opportunities. The event was such a blast, the next day the social media sites were posting red carpet snapshots like crazy. Presently, there's talk of a second round of the magazine release party.

SDM Magazine Release Party

Atlanta rapper T.I. dropped in at Walmart to surprises families and kids with Christmas gifts. He asked shoppers what did they need and that was it. Kids grabbed everything from Xbox's to power wheel trucks. Some checkout prices ranged from $400 to $1000, but Santa was in the building to cover the cost.

T.I. is always a person to help his community. He figures if his fans can go out and online to buy his music in stores he can also show support to them by helping out at Christmas time.

T.I.

The Return of Scarface

STANLEY L. BATTLE WRITES A CLASSIC GANGSTER NOVEL ABOUT THE RETURN OF A CRIMINAL ICON AND HIS EMPIRE.

by Cheraee C.

Have you ever thought about their being a continuation to the 1993 Thriller Scarface? Mocy Publishing presents "The Son of Scarface" - Part 1 which is the literary sequel to the movie Scarface. This book is phenomenal and well-detailed as the author captures every experience, memory, and scene with conviction. The author uses a symbolic language that is hip and original. Most importantly, this book takes place in Detroit. If you are into books that feature heavy content with every type of drug you can imagine, the most violent scenes, mobster affiliations, and conniving ways, The Son of Scarface - Part 1 is definitely a book you should add to your gangster library.

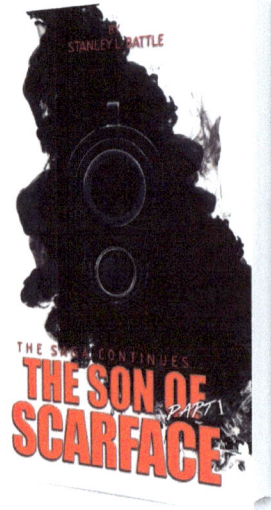

The Son of Scarface Part 1
By Stanley L. Battle

Available from Amazon.com and other online stores

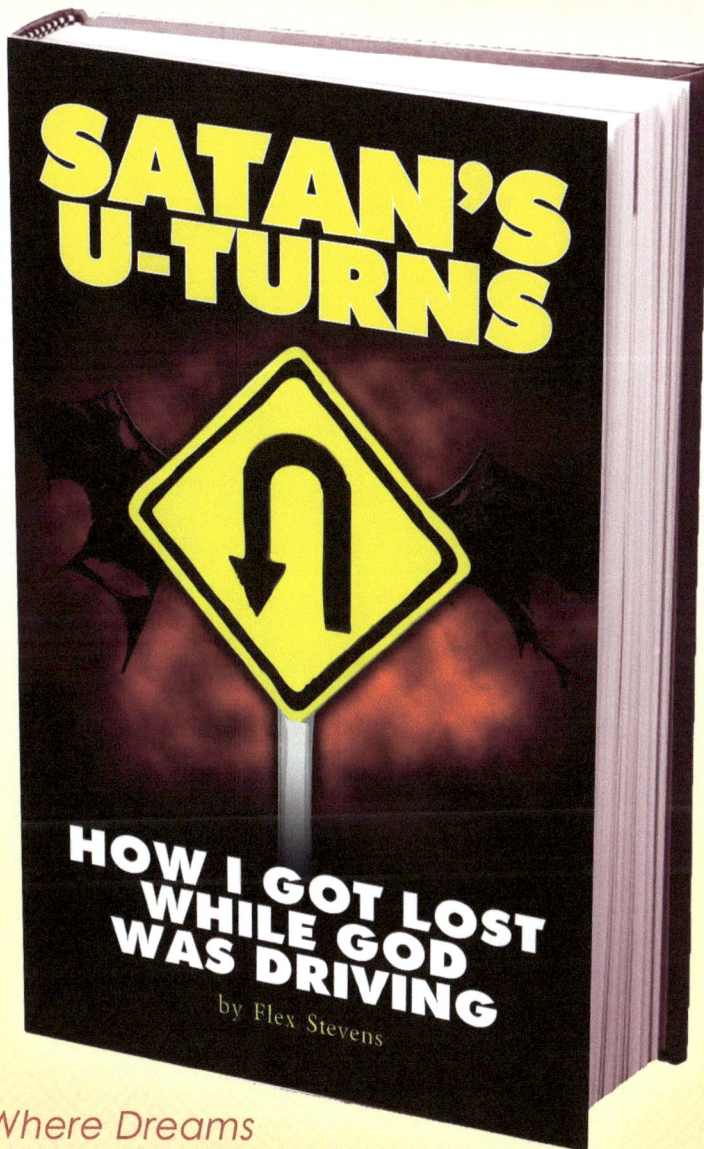

Kosta Hits The Lottery

DETROIT'S OWN KOSTA RELEASES AN ALBUM WITH INSTRUCTIONS TO OTHER ARTISTS ON HOW TO DO IT YOURSELF .

by Cheraee C.

A contemporary rapper orchestrating that hip hop with a twist is a hip hop aspirant by the name of Kosta. Originating from the westside of Detroit, Kosta is full of ambition. Rapping since 2006, Kosta is an unsigned artist determined to make a name for himself. His lyrics are straightforward, his delivery is smooth, and his music is full of content.

Kosta is a solo artist, but he is also apart of a group called "Daiwao" which stands for defined as individuals we are one. His first solo project is titled "D.I.Y" which is abbreviated for Do it Yourself and was released October 2015. Some popular singles from the EP include "Carry On," "Lottery," and "Zonin." Kosta's banger "Lottery" is featured on the Support Detroit Movement Compilation Album Vol.1. Throughout Detroit, Kosta

has collaborated with some local Detroit artists including KevforPrez, TJ Upshaw, and Oba Rowland. His music is available on iTunes, Spotify, Google Play, YouTube, and Soundcloud just to name a few.

In the new year, Kosta plans to keep branding himself, release his second solo project, and plan a promotional tour. You can stay connected to Kosta on Facebook @Kosta Kazanova, and on Instagram and Twitter @Kostaf2d.

R&B is back with Ishmaelsoul

PROCLAMING TO BRING SOULFUL MUSIC BACK MR. ISHMAELSOUL SINGS SWEET MUSIC WHILE GAINING NATIONAL EXPOSER.

by Cheraee C.

When you hear soul, it must be the R&B phenomenon from the D, ready to take over the music industry. IshmaelSoul is a R&B singer, a producer, a songwriter, a ghost-writer, and an artist manager along with many other musical attributes. In addition to that, he is the CEO and founder of his own label called Unified Records which he started in 2013. He also does vocal arrangements, hooks, and features on tracks. Ishmael is a diverse artist, but he mainly sings R&B and hip hop. Gracing stages worldwide, citywide Ishmael has performed at Hart Plaza, MGM Grand, Motor City Casino, and Greektown Casino. Some big names he has blessed the stage with include Deelishis, Jay O'Neal, and Ray Ray.

In the past, Ishmael was signed to Boss Network and Sony, but he still has close ties with both labels. In 2011, he released his first project titled "Ishmael." Early 2016, he plans to release his second project titled "Soul Anatomy." His current singles are "My Enemy" and a song called "Right Rib" produced by Helluva and Lyriq. Presently, you can listen to Ishmael's music on Reverbnation, but when he drops his second album his music will be available in all digital music stores.

In 2016, you can look forward to Ishmael touring and performing all over the U.S. He is heavily promoted and constantly receiving bookings by Lamonte McClore from Chi-Town. Stay connected with Ishmael on Facebook @Ishmael Melton and on Instagram and Twitter @Ishmaelsoul.

ABSOLUT. EMPIRE.

YaBigg Dawg Blast Movement

THE STREET HITTA DJ MOVEMENT IS IN FULL EFFECT WITH THE CAPTAIN OF THE SHIP BIGG DAWG BLAST.

Photography by Cheraee C.

An eminent DJ from the D's radio station FM 98 WJLB, making noise with his brand new movement is DJ Bigg Dawg Blast. With over 20 years in the business, Big Blast is the CEO and innovator of a brand new coalition he calls "Street Hitta DJs." His main purpose is to help new artists breakthrough the industry. It's clear that the success of an artist starts in the streets. When street fame is intact, an artist is more marketable for radio play.

On January 20, 2016, Blast will be launching his new campaign at his Street Hitta DJs launch party. The launch party will be the start of a chain of events representing his movement. In March 2016, he plans to release a mixtape called "Heat in the Streets Vol.1." The mixtape will contain a variety of underground music that is cutting-edge and captivating. In April 2016, he plans to have a next to blow showcase where he will let aspiring artists show off their musical skills on the center stage. The winner of the showcase will get Street Hitta DJs to work their record in the streets for five consecutive weeks. In June 2016, he plans to have a promotional tour ranging all over the Midwest because his movement isn't limited to local recognition. Another objective is to get DJs all over the country involved with upcoming artists from their city as well. It doesn't take anything, but a hit for a DJ to play a song. What does a DJ have to lose from exploring new talent, besides being creditable for that new talent.

On New Year's Day, the official website www.streethittadjs.com will be available. Stay connected to

BIG DAWG BLAST PRESENTS

JAN. 20TH 2016 WEDNESDAY

The Official STREET HITTA DJ'S Launch Party

WITH SPECIAL PERFORMANCES BY

ICEWEAR VEZZO   NEISHA NASHAE   TEAM 734   ERICA CANNON

"WE TAKEN OVER THE STREETS"

HAZEL'S PLACE
5516 MICHIGAN AVE, DETROIT, MI

DOORS OPEN AT 9PM - $10 ENTRY BEFORE 10PM

GRAPHIC DESIGNS BY: WWW.NEWVISIONMEDIALLC.COM

Blast and his movement on Instagram @streethittadjs and on Instagram and Twitter @biggdawgblast as well.

Pandora Trouble

MAJOR RECORD LABELS SUE PANDORA OVER ALLEGATIONS THAT PANDORA NEVER PAID OUT ROYALTIES.

by Semaja Turner

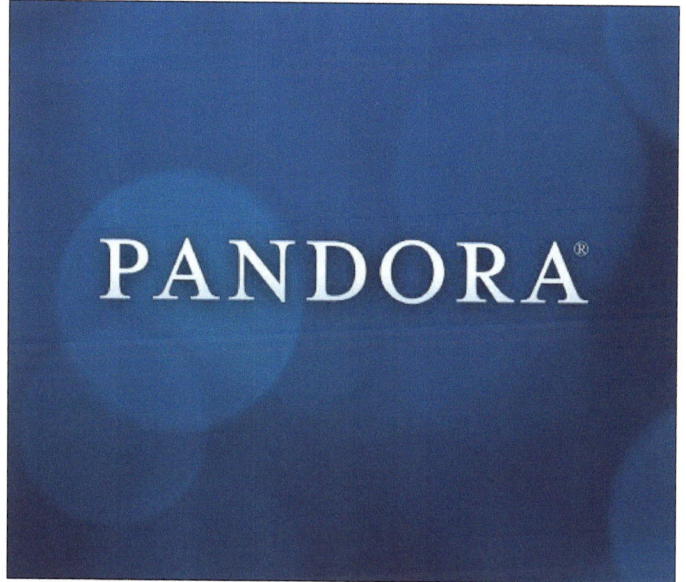

As expected, major record labels, and the RIAA filed a copyright infringement lawsuit last month in New York state court against Pandora for streaming recordings without making any royalty payments to labels and copyright owners. This lawsuit is a followed by one filed against SiriusXM in September 2014.

Record labels are seeking to take action to SiriusXM over their music. The labels say that both digital music services took advantage of the copyright loopholes, since the master recording for copyright wasn't created federally until 1972. Although, the labels claim that their master recordings are protected by individual state copyright laws and, therefore, deserve royalty payments.

SoundExchange CEO and President Michael Huppe said the estimates for non-payment for pre-1972 recordings would earn the artists and labels $60 million in royalties of non-payment in 2013 alone.

The Voice is High Upon a Cloud

THE QUEEN OF R&B TRAP NEISHA NESHAE IS TAKING THE MUSIC INDUSTRY BY STORM AND ITS ALL OR NOTHING

by Cheraee C.

With a regal voice circulating through airwaves across the nation; it's a pleasure to have a female artist like Neisha Neshae grace the music forefront. Blooming from the south side of Ypsilanti, Neisha Neshae is a thoroughbred artist with a powerful story. A lot of odds were against her, but the queen of R&B trap is winning now that she uses music as a mirror for her life.

Neisha's style is trill, savvy, and neoteric. Bringing a new genre of music to the industry, Neisha Neshae is the trendsetter of R&B trap. R&B trap is a mellifluous fusion of rapping and singing. Neisha also composes her own music writing lyrics that are bossy, ear-gripping, and prevailing.

Dropping December 31, 2015 on New Year's Eve is Neisha's first EP titled "What the Streets been Missing." The mixtape includes the radio banger "On a Cloud," "All or Nothing" featuring Mack Nickels,."Boss Up," "Hood Love" and more dope, appealing songs. Neisha's music is available on iTunes, Spotify, Google Play, and all major internet music stores. You can also check out YouTube and Soundcloud for many song features from Neisha collaborating with an array of many local Detroit artists. Neisha is currently signed to TandB Music Group, but who knows what million dollar record deal the future has in store for this gifted star.

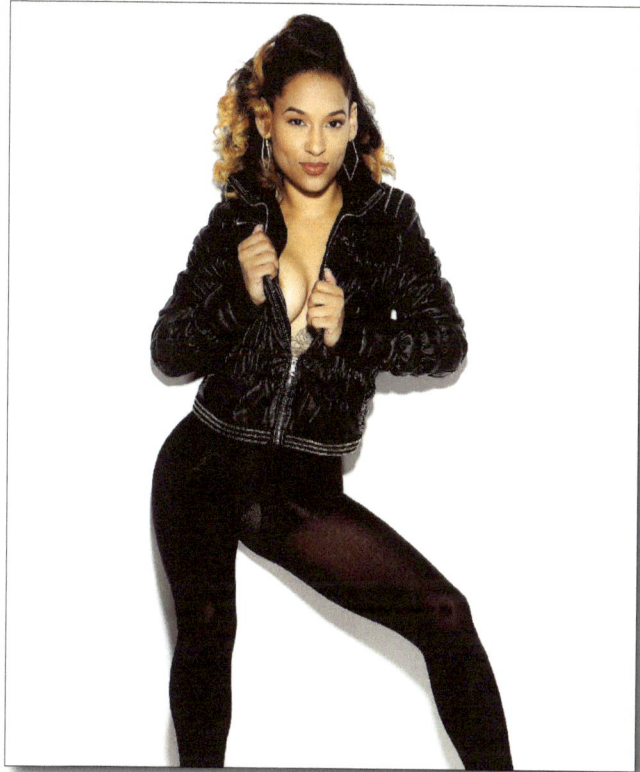

Neisha is a firm example of why you should use your past as positive ammunition. You never know what you can become if you believe in yourself or how you can influence the world with your story. Adopted into a childhood of abuse, loss, anger, and free-spiritedness, you can't help but to respect her hustle. In life it's easy to lose yourself, but once you inline your focus with your dreams, the sky is the limit. Besides the release of her mixtape on December 31st, she will be opening the show for the King of R&B R.Kelly at the Fox Theatre, Detroit MI.

To stay connected to Neisha Neshae, you can follow her on Instagram @Neishaneshae, Facebook @Neisha Ne'shae, and Twitter @NeishaNeshae. You can also visit her website www.iamneisha.com. If you thought Neisha had everybody "On a Cloud" in 2015, wait to see what she has planned for 2016.

TOP 10 CHARTS

TOP 10 DIGITAL SINGLES AND ALBUMS
JANUARY 1, 2016

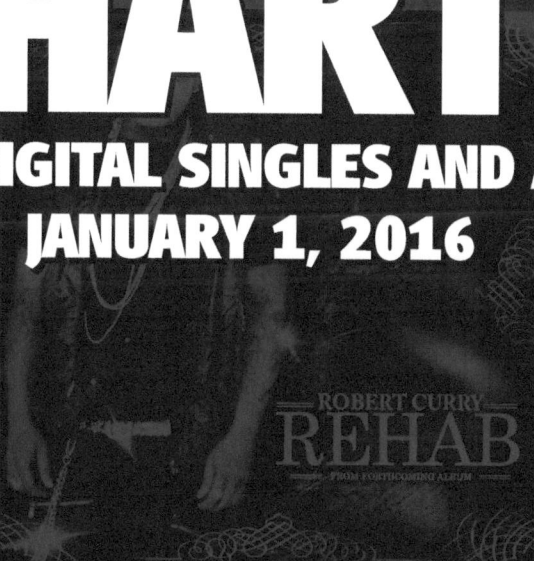

TOP 10 CHARTS

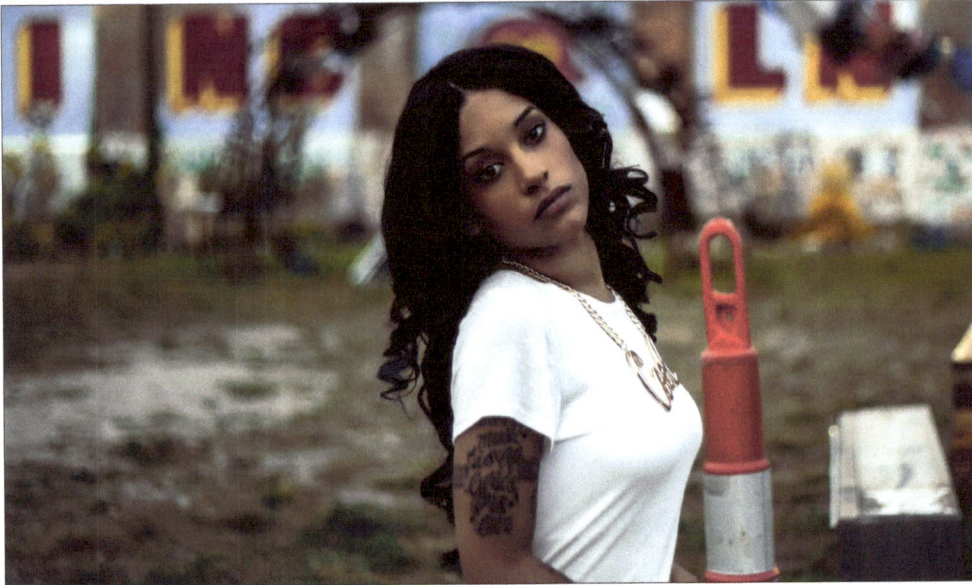

NEISHA NESHAE - GET'S HIGH UPON A CLOUD AND EVERYONE IS RIDING THE WAVE.

TOP 10 SINGLES
CHART OF THE MONTH

No.	Artist - Song Title
1	NEISHA NESHAE - ON A CLOUD
2	TYRESE - SHAME
3	ESKO - MEAN SOMETHING
4	KENDRICK LAMAR - ALRIGHT
5	KOSTA - LOTTERY
6	T.I. - PRIVATE SHOW FT. CHRIS BROWN
7	CHIEF 313 - WHY TRY
8	DRAKE - HOTLINE BLING
9	LYNN CARTER - TOO LITTLE
10	RICH MOOK - YES I DO

TOP 10 ALBUMS
CHART OF THE MONTH

No.	Artist - Album Title
1	TYRESE - BLACK ROSE
2	TY DOLLA $IGN - FREE TC
3	THE WEEKND - BEAUTY BEHIND THE MADNESS
4	JANET - UNBREAKABLE
5	DRAKE & FUTURE - WHAT A TIME TO BE ALIVE
6	AYE MONEY - SDM COMPILATION (VOLUME 2)
7	FETTY WAP - FETTY WAP
8	THE GAME - THE DOCUMENTARY 2
9	J. COLE - 2014 FOREST HILLS DRIVE
10	DRAKE - IF YOU'RE READING THIS IT'S TOO LATE

TOP #1

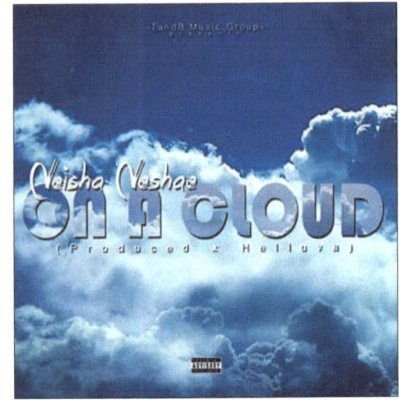

Neisha Neshae
On a Cloud

Coming in at #1 this month, *Neisha Neshae* breaks the charts with the single *"On a Cloud"*. It's just a sample of her new album which is due to drop this month.

Black Rose

ARTIST: Tyrese
REVIEWER: Casino B.
RATING: 5

TOP 3 ALBUMS THIS MONTH

Tyrese never expected to be a superstar recording artist. Things changed dramatically when he joined a supergroup, TGT, with Tank and Ginuwine. After things went left with the group Tyrese begin recording a solo project titled Black Rose. It took over 17 years to release the album, but Tyrese finally created a classic love and soul album. Black Rose is Tyrese's first hit album that is climbing charts in all countries. After listening to the album, I would say, Tyrese Gibson has finally come to life.

The album also features many producers including Rockwilder, B.A.M., Warryn "Baby Dub" Campbell, and Harvey Mason Jr., as well as co-writers Eric Hudson, Ambrosius, Tim Kelley, Snoop Dogg, Davion Farris, Christopher Perry, Marcus Hodge, Kenyon and Andrew Dixon. The single "Shame" is one of his breakout hits that went viral upon release. Bottomline, the album get five stars.

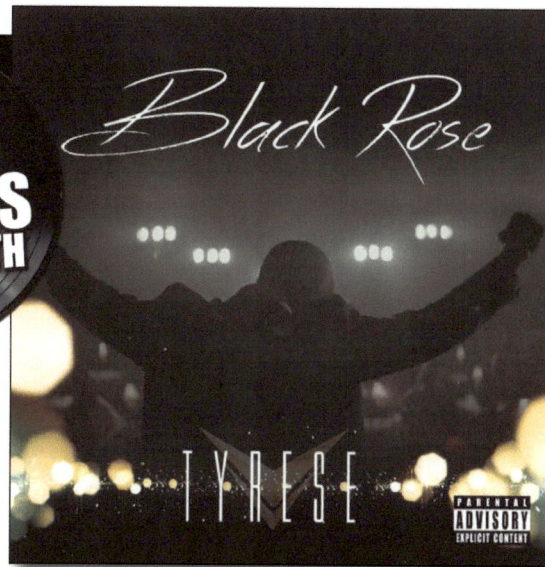

RATE METER: 1 - WACK 2 - NEEDS WORK 3 - STRAIGHT 4 - BANGER 5 - CLASSIC

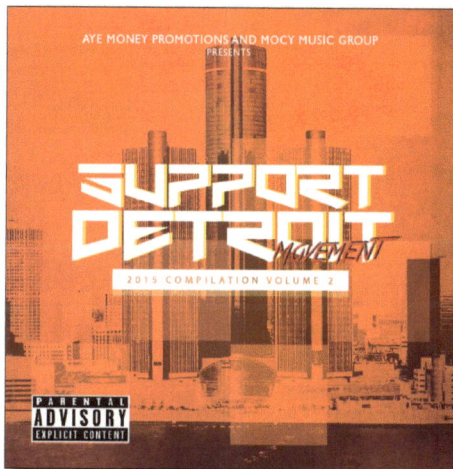

SDM Compilation Vol. 2

ARTIST: Aye Money
REVIEWER: Motowndiva
RATING: 4

SDM Vol. 2 is a mixtape filled with local talents, from rap to r&b. The mixtape is hosted by the promo king Aye Money. This album is well put together and certified as a banger. When I listen to the track "Mean Something" by Esko, I thought it was Future. The album deserves a gold plaque.

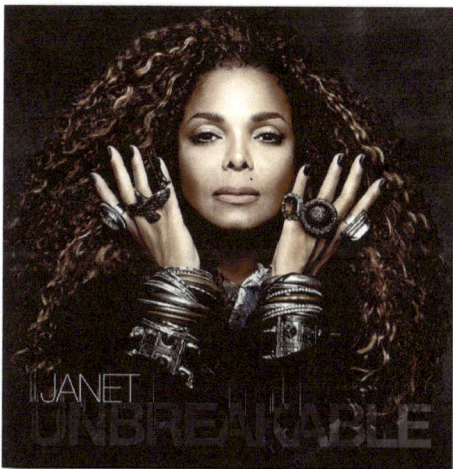

Unbreakable

ARTIST: Janet
REVIEWER: Cheraee C.
RATING: 4

Janet Jackson always comes with the best each and every performance. On the track "The Great Forever", Janet channeled her brother the great Michael Jackson. Thanks to the duo Jimmy Jam and Terry Lewis, Unbreakable will now be added to Janet's collection of hit records.

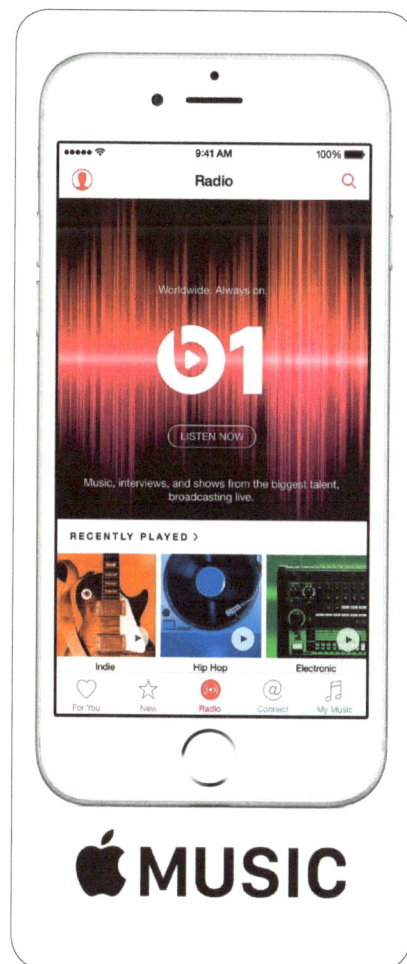

HEELS &
SKILLZ

Daija
is a native
Detroiter and a
gorgeous perfume
model who enjoys
modeling.

Photography by
@Terance Drake

HEELS &
SKILLZ

Pocahontaz

a rap artist who enjoys writing, recording & performing music.

instagram
@Imjust_Poca_=

Photography by
@Juan TheGvImage

HEELS & SKILLZ

Ebony

is a beautiful,
part-time model
from Pontiac, MI
who works at GM.

Sweet Sensation
HOW THIS DETROITER IS SPREADING SWEET JOY IN THE METRO AREA.
by Cheraee C.

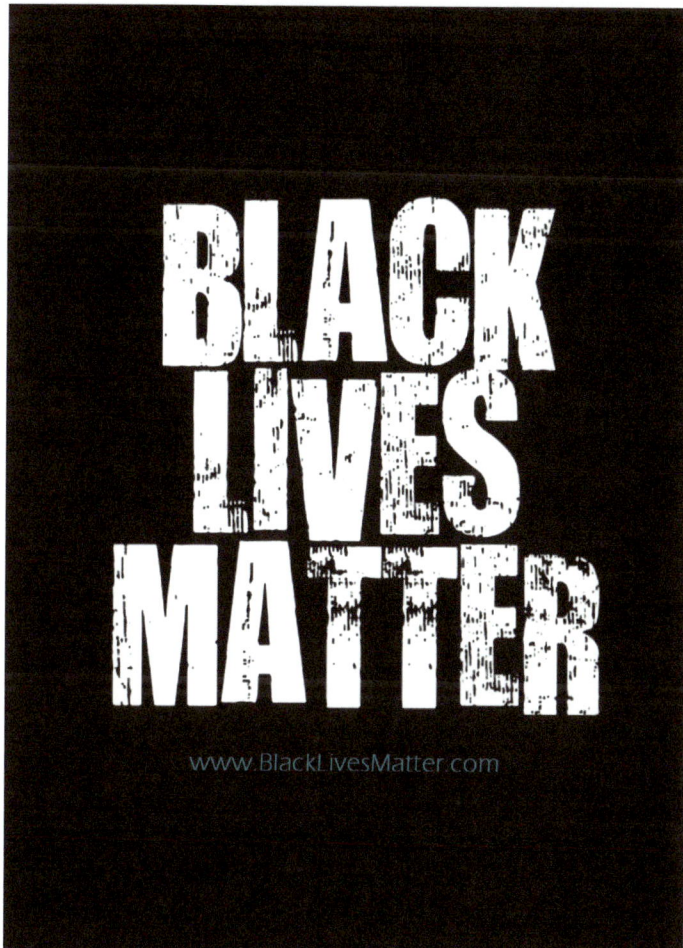

Q is a 38-year-old native Detroiter who is the proud owner of a mobile dessert buffet business she and her daughters' launched in 2013. Currently, they work in downtown Detroit, Michigan near Campus Martius. Since 2013, they've been blessed to host events at the African Wright Museum, the Music Hall, and the Jazz Festival. Q hosts fashion shows, banquets, and receptions, but loves fashion shows the most. Their design ideas come as we speak with our clients and we listen to what it is their looking to see and accomplish at their event and we make it happen.

"I'm a proud mother of four beautiful daughters' and I'm honored to be an example on how to step out on faith, trust GOD, and work hard toward achieving your dreams. I also have a non-profit organization with a partnership between pastors' and business owners'. They work together and marry ideas in an effort to empower our people in a successful direction no matter what their setback is. I'm honored to have met Mr. Casino. He is the most gentle and sincere man I've ever met. I thank him for his sincere efforts in wanting us to work together and become successful!"

NEXT 2 BLOW

EVERYTHING IS AUHMAZ!N WITH THE NEW YOUNG ARTIST FROM DETROIT MICHIGAN.

A new female MC thriving from the eastside of Detroit is an upcoming artist Auhmaz!n. She's a rapper, a songwriter, and an author. The genre that represents her music is hip hop. With a sound that is distinct and fresh, she is an unsigned artist, but rest insure she won't be unsigned for long.

Her latest singles include "Take My Place," "Bob Marley Good," and her (Big Sean) "Paradise Freestyle." Down south her single "Bob Marley Good" is a radio banger all over 105.7 and Mississippi radio. In 2016, Auhmaz!n plans to release two songs she collaborated on alongside T Ray and M-City JR. During the summer of 2016, Auhmaz!n plans to release her first album "Born to be the Greatest." Listen to Auhmaz!n's music on YouTube, Soundcloud, and www.23fosho.com.

Besides being an artist, Auhmaz!n is talented in all areas of fine arts. In 2011, Auhmaz!n released a poetry book titled "Shatters of My Broken Heart." Her book contains a selection of her greatest poems and is available on www.authorhouse.co.uk. In 2016, Auhmaz!n plans to officially launch her own t-shirt line called "Everything is Auhmaz!n." She currently rocks her t-shirts in her music videos, promo videos, and events/shows.

You can follow her on Facebook @ Princeauhmazin R Wright, and on Instagram and Twitter @_Auhmaz!n_.

Photography by
@A List Photography

The country bumpkin and military brat straight out of Houston, Texas who gets plenty Detroit love is Mz. Platium. Mz. Platium is a rapper, singer, and songwriter who has her dope music coasting throughout 15 states and three countries. At this moment she is signed to Queens With Purpose. She is more than just an artist because she doesn't limit herself to just one single genre of music. Mz. Platium makes pop, hip-hop, R&B, and gospel music. In the past, she has worked radio for 88.1, been a TV host at WPHR, and done some modeling.

In the summer of 2016, Mz. Platium will be releasing her anticipated album "Look At Me Now." She is currently in the process of shooting the videos for two exclusive singles from her album titled "You Can Go" and "Woosa." Her music is currently available on www.bandcamp.com, but in the future, she plans to market her music all over the internet. Besides musically, Mz. Platium has other ventures that are bound to take her to the top. She is a global performer that has traveled the world performing with countless mainstream artists from the U.S. to overseas. In the summer of 2016, she plans to release her own perfume called "Ice-de-neia." In 2017, she will be releasing a film titled "Breaking Into The Business." Mz. Platium has dwelled in the music industry for 14 years so she has a lot of lessons and insight she wants to share with the world.

To stay connected with Mz. Platium and her endeavors, you can follow her on Facebook @Cantera Daheat, on Twitter @canetrawoods, and on Instagram @mzplatium. You can also download the iheart Radio app and add her radio station lil-lady.

Mz. Platium

KidJay

KidJay is a fly upcoming rapper from Ypsilanti, MI. He is an independent artist who's been promoting his music for 2 years, songwriting, and hosting shows for charity events. As a rapper, his music is respectable and censored. His main goal is to show society that you can make good music without equating profanity in your lyrics.

In October 2015, KidJay released his first mixtape titled "True Facts" which is available on Soundcloud. Kid Jay's hit single "Better Be" is featured on the Support Detroit Movement compilation album Vol.1. Some future singles he plans to release in 2016 include "Inspiration," and "Fake it to you Make it." You can listen to KidJay's music on Soundcloud @KidJaydaprince and on YouTube.

In 2016, he plans to release new, hotter material and more mixtapes. Stay connected to KidJay and like his Facebook artist page @KidJay, on Instagram @officialkidjay, and on Twitter @realkidjay15.

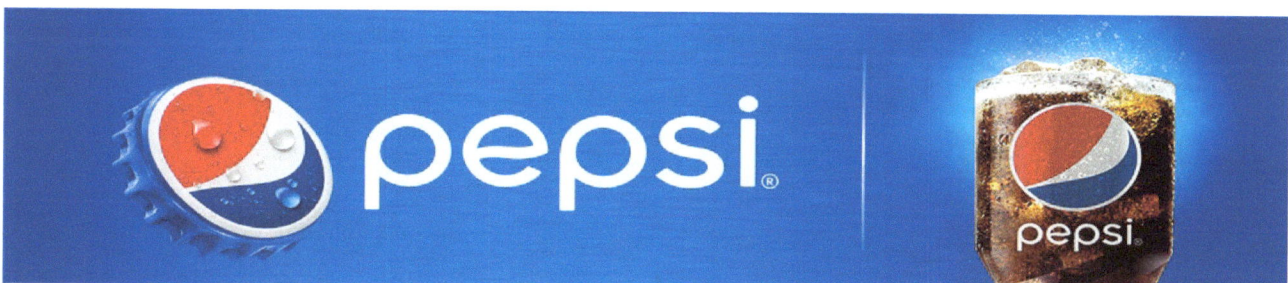

SNAP SHOTS

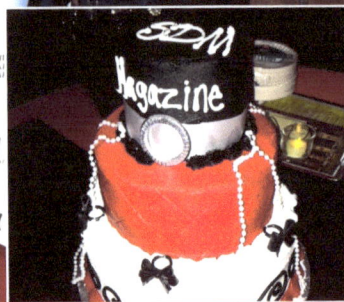

Email Your Snap Shots to
snapshots@sdmlive.com

Red Carpet

WE HAVE THE LOWEST PRINTING PRICES IN THE NATION

250 EVENT TICKETS

FULL-COLOR ON BOTH SIDES ON THICK UV COATED 14 PT

only $45

1000 BUSINESS CARDS

FULL-COLOR ON BOTH SIDES ON THICK UV COATED 14 PT

only $25

1000 4X6 CLUB FLYERS

FULL-COLOR ON BOTH SIDES ON THICK UV COATED 14 PT

only $65

Need a Design? Add $20 for Business Card or $40 for Flyer

2x5ft VINYL BANNER

FULL-COLOR IN or OUTDOOR BANNER w/GROMMETS

only $99

5000 BUSINESS CARDS

FULL-COLOR ON BOTH SIDES ON THICK UV COATED 14 PT

only $99

2500 4X6 CLUB FLYERS

FULL-COLOR ON BOTH SIDES ON THICK UV COATED 14 PT

only $85

CHECK OUT MORE SPECIALS & ORDER ONLINE ANYTIME: WWW.5DSPRODUCTIONS.COM

1.888.718.2999 5DS PRODUCTIONS® THE PRINT MEDIA CENTER.

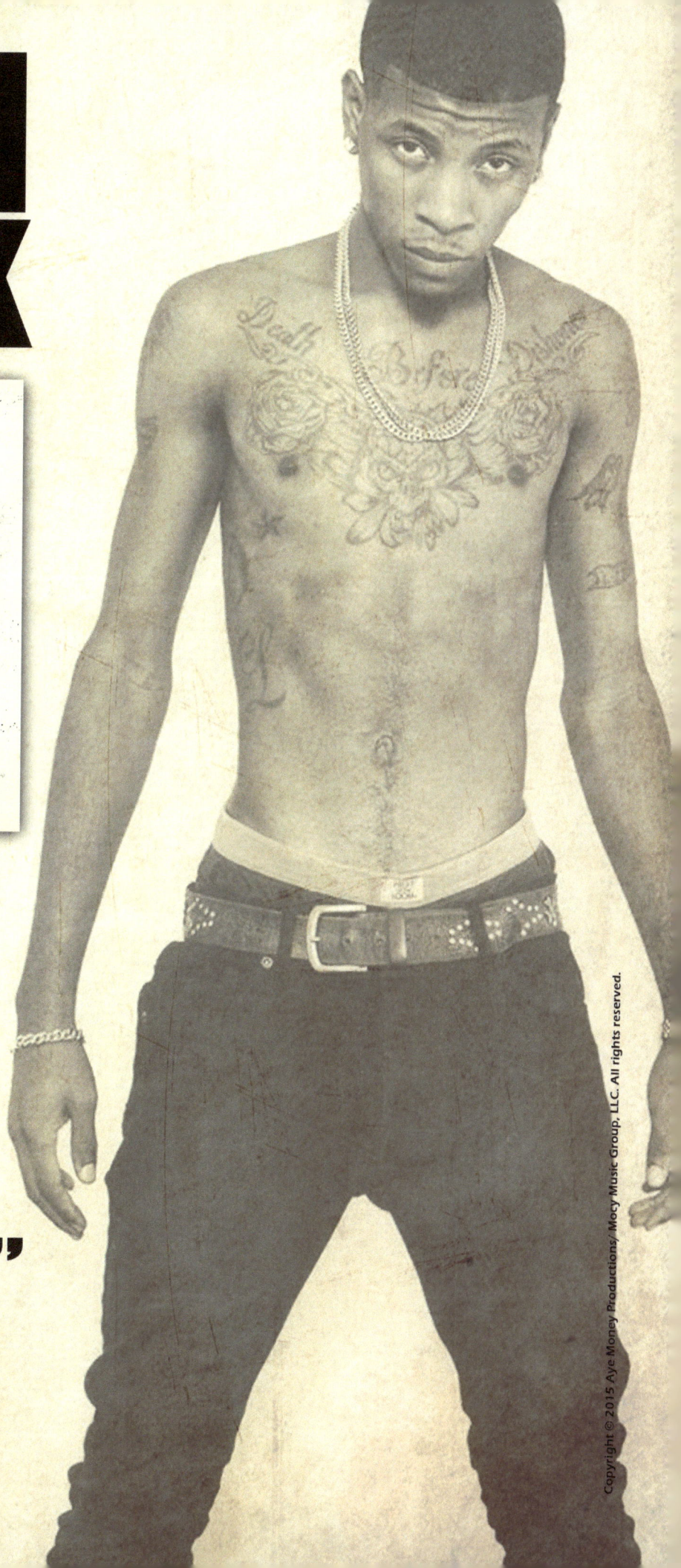

THE ALL NEW STYLE OF MAGAZINE-BOOKS

SDM

www.ingramcontent.com/pod-product-compliance
Lightning Source LLC
Chambersburg PA
CBHW040019050426
42452CB00002B/53